POEMS
POEMAS

Coral Bracho

POEMS
POEMAS

poetry translation centre

First published by Enitharmon Press, 2008
Published by The Poetry Translation Centre Ltd, 2010
PO Box 61051
London SE16 4YY

www.poetrytranslation.org

Poems © Coral Bracho, 2008
Translations from the Spanish © Katherine Pierpoint and Tom Boll
Introduction © Tom Boll

ISBN: 978-0-9560576-3-1

The Poetry Translation Centre gratefully acknowledges the financial
support of Arts Council England.

'Of Their Eyes Adorned with Crystal Sands'
has been published in *The Wolf*.

British Library Cataloguing-in-Publication Data.
A catalogue record for this book is available
from the British Library.

Designed in Albertina by Libanus Press
and printed in Great Britain by
MPG Books Group, Bodmin and King's Lynn

Contents

Introduction	6
Of Their Eyes Adorned with Crystal Sands	9
Far-off Settlements	13
Veins of Salt	15
From this Light	17
Thread in a Spider's Web	21
Wasp on Water	23
Marks of Time	25
Behind the Curtain	27
Water of Jellyfish	29

Introduction

Born in Mexico City in 1951, Coral Bracho first came to prominence thirty years ago with two collections, *Peces de piel fugaz* (*Fish of Fleeting Skin*, 1977) and *El ser que va a morir* (*The Being that Is Going to Die*, 1982). She appears in the aftermath of the great political and pseudo-religious projects of the earlier twentieth-century avant-garde. In their place she offers something more modest yet no less rewarding: a poetic world that is sensual and exploratory, attentive to the intermittencies of the individual's experience.

The sensuality of Bracho's poetry makes for an easy point of access. The opening poem of this selection, 'Of Their Eyes Adorned with Crystal Sands', carefully builds up a visual scene of temple, sculpture and acanthus shade, which is intensified by appeals to the other senses: the 'warm' leaves of the almond trees, and 'lovely smells; of stooked-up corn'. We are drawn in physically to the site of some ancient ritual. But where are the people? Vividly realised yet also curiously deserted, the tableau is suffused with a troubling intimation of vacancy.

Human relationships remain a pivotal element of Bracho's work, but they appear fleetingly. Whether the sight of a lover in 'Thread in a Spider's Web', or the reassuring 'warm, firm' hands of 'From this Light', human contact is grasped against the background of a physical world in constant flux. 'Marks of Time', another of the poems from her fourth collection, *La voluntad del ámbar* (*The Will of Amber*, 1998), provides the most recognisably autobiographical, and poignant, example of this scenario. Here the poet recalls a childhood visit with her father to a mine. As the young girl revels in her father's 'bright gaze', she takes in the surrounding rocky landscape, transferring it as metaphor to the 'clouds of quartz, and flint, up high'. Yet the permanence of rock on earth is just an appearance in the sky, an effect of light created by a declining sun that will leave the poem's protagonists in darkness.

If 'Marks of Time' reveals a strong elegiac undertow to Bracho's work, her preoccupation with the shifting manifestations of light and water can have a more celebratory aspect. Wallace Stevens memorably described death as 'the mother of beauty', a source of loss but also of momentary vision caught on the wing. We have chosen to conclude with Bracho's *tour de force* of delighted observation, 'Water of Jellyfish'. When she read for the Poetry Translation Centre in 2005, she described the poem as an attempt 'to get close to the movement of water'. A great teeming succession of liquid images, it is a poem to be enjoyed rather than interpreted.

Bracho's Spanish covers a wide range from the barest colloquial phrase to intricate syntactic construction. The less flexible word order of English inevitably provided a barrier to some of these effects. Nevertheless, Katherine Pierpoint has consistently and ingeniously found engaging English form for Spanish that can, beguilingly, be concrete yet also suggestive. We offer these translations in the hope that English readers will encounter familiar pleasures, but also the more uncertain areas of experience that Bracho explores.

TOM BOLL

DE SUS OJOS ORNADOS DE ARENAS VÍTREAS

Desde la exhalación de estos peces de mármol,
desde la suavidad sedosa
de sus cantos,
de sus ojos ornados
de arenas vítreas,
la quietud de los templos y los jardines

(en sus sombras de acanto, en la piedras
que tocan y reblandecen)

    han abierto sus lechos,
    han fundado sus cauces
    bajo las hojas tibias de los almendros.

Dicen del tacto
de sus destellos,
de los juegos tranquilos que deslizan al borde,
a la orilla lenta de los ocasos.
De sus labios de hielo.

Ojos de piedras finas.

De la espuma que arrojan, del aroma que vierten

(En los atrios: las velas, los amarantos.)

sobre el ara levísima de las siembras.

    (Desde el templo:
    el perfume de las espigas,
    las escamas,
    los ciervos. Dicen de sus reflejos.)

OF THEIR EYES ADORNED WITH CRYSTAL SANDS

From the outbreath of these fish made of marble,
from the silken stroke
of their slim sides,
their eyes touched
with crystal sands,
the quiet of the temples and gardens

(in their acanthus shade, in the stones
they touch and blend with)

    they have opened their beds,
    have made their own wet ways
    under the almond trees' warm leaves.

They tell of the touch
of this light,
of that quiet interplay sliding at the edge of things,
at the slow edge of sunsets.
From their freezing lips.

Eyes of precious stone.

From the fine spray they throw off, and fragrances

(In the halls: the candle-light, the amaranth's unfading flower.)

onto the altar, light as a touch, when it's time to sow the seeds.

    (From the temple:
    lovely smells; of stooked-up corn,
    fish-scales,
    stags and does. They tell of what is given back in reflection.)

En las noches,
el mármol frágil de su silencio,
el preciado tatuaje, los trazos limpios

    (han ahogado la luz
    a la orilla; en la arena)

sobre la imagen tersa,
sobre la ofrenda inmóvil
de las praderas.

Night-times
their delicate marble-stony silence
with their precious crazings, clean contours

    (they have flooded out the light
    at the shoreline, in the sands)

upon that sheer image,
upon the harvest gifts
from the meadows.

POBLACIONES LEJANAS

Sus relieves candentes, sus pasajes, son un salmo
luctuoso y monocorde;
los niños corren y gritan,
como pequeños lapsos, en un eterno, enmudecido
sepia demente. Hay ciudades, también,
que dulcifican la luz del sol:
En sus espejos de oro crepuscular las aguas abren y encienden
cercos de aromas y caricias rituales; en sus baños:
las risas, las paredes reverdecientes
—Sus templos beben del mar.

Vagos lindes desiertos (Las caravanas, los vendavales, las
    noches combas y despobladas, las tardes lentas,
son arenas franqueables que las separan) mirajes, ecos que las enturbian,
que las empalman;
un gusto líquido a sal en las furtivas comisuras;
Y esta evocada resonancia.

FAR-OFF SETTLEMENTS

Their burning, hot-branded outlines, their inner pathways, are all a psalm
sung sad and monotonous;
children run and yell
like little blips, in never-ending quiet,
demented sepia. And there are also cities
which can make this sun's light sweet:
In their dusky golden looking-glasses, water breaks, and lights up
those gathered sweet smells and old caresses; in the warm bathing-places:
the laughter, the walls turning green now once again.
– Their temples sip from the seas.

Ghostly city limits, wavering (The caravans, the strong south winds, the
over-arching nights with no-one there, the long afternoons –
what separates all these are the untrodden sands), mirages, echoes that
    cloud them,
that connect them;
a sly wet lick of salt in the corners of the mouth;
And this resonance, called forth.

HEBRAS DE SAL

Viento y piedra
se funden, agua y viento
en un reino fluido
y subterráneo. Sus corrientes se cierran
en estanques profundos. Ecos que en ellos giran
y se reflejan. Voces
que se concentran. Sobre el lecho de un tiempo dúctil
y primigenio
vuelcan un mineral de soles líquidos.
Dejan hebras
de sal.

VEINS OF SALT

Wind and stone blend,
water and wind
in a flowing
underworld. Their currents converge
in deep pools. Echoes spin there
and reflect back. Voices
gather. Along the riverbed of time,
so pliable, and primitive,
they strew their minerals; liquid suns.
They leave their veins
of salt.

DESDE ESTA LUZ

Desde esta luz en que incide, con delicada
flama,
la eternidad. Desde este jardín atento,
desde esta sombra.
Abre su umbral al tiempo,
y en él se imantan
los objetos.
Se ahondan en él,
y él los sostiene y los ofrece así:
claros, rotundos,
generosos. Frescos y llenos de su alegre volumen,
de su esplendor festivo,
de su hondura estelar.
Sólidos y distintos
alían su espacio
y su momento, su huerto exacto
para ser sentidos. Como piedras precisas
en un jardín. Como lapsos trazados
sobre un templo.

Una puerta, una silla,
el mar.
La blancura profunda,
desfasada
del muro. Las líneas breves
que lo centran.
Deja el tamarindo un fulgor
entre la noche espesa.

FROM THIS LIGHT

That delicate flame –
eternity –
is falling, slanting, on this light. From this garden, so composed;
from this shadow.
Eternity lifts its latch onto time
and, there in it, objects
are magnetised.
They sink themselves in deeper,
and it holds them, then renders them back like this:
very clear, full,
abundant. Breezy, brim-ful of their own sunny selves,
their festival glory,
deep space.
Solid and separate,
they bring places,
time and space together, those neat little gardens,
so that we can feel them fully. Like perfectly-placed stones
in a garden. Like time's blueprint,
overlaid on a temple.

A doorway, a seat,
the sea.
The very old, deep
whiteness
of a wall. The slim lines,
all pointing into it.
The tamarind tree stands, glowing
through the dark.

Suelta el cántaro el ruido
solar del agua.
Y la firme tibieza de sus manos; deja la noche densa,
la noche vasta y desbordada sobre el hondo caudal,
su entrañable
tibieza.

The water-jug lets stream
the water's own sound, of the sun.
And his hands; warm, firm; the night, tangible,
night vast and brimming over, a profound river-flow,
his intimate, deep
warmth.

HILO EN UNA TELA DE ARAÑA

Un arroyo imantado por la brisa y la luz,
un transcurrir cobrizo es el hilo que fluye
en la tela de araña. Charcos de plata cambian
de unas hojas a otras, de unas huellas
a otras sobre la tierra blanda. Te veo cruzar
entre dos líneas. Lo amo,
digo.
Entre dos ramas del azar
fluye el arroyo,
su hilo hechizado por el mar de la luz,
por el licor
de su corriente. Es el agua que embriaga
el atardecer. Es el fuego que fluye
sin cesar hacia el este.   Bajo su fiel
solar
te pienso.

THREAD IN A SPIDER'S WEB

A little stream, drawn by the magnets of air and light,
and flowing like time, like copper forming,
is the thread
in a spider's web. Pools of silver shimmer
from one leaf to another, from one path trodden
to another on the soft ground. I see you go across, over there,
between two lines. 'I love him',
I say.
The little stream forks; flows between
two possibilities.
Its thread is in thrall to this sea of light,
this liquid,
coursing. This water makes the evening sing, heady
and drunk. Its fire flows
on into the east forever.   Held in the sun's
fine balance
I think of you.

UNA AVISPA SOBRE EL AGUA

La superficie del agua es tensa
para una avispa,
es un sendero múltiple fluyendo siempre
como el tacto del tiempo
sobre la hondura quieta
de un corto espacio.

Corto es el tiempo
en que flota; corta
la distancia en que gira
por incesantes laberintos,
remolinos inciertos, llamas,
y transparencia
inextricable.

WASP ON WATER

The water surface holds, tense,
for a wasp;
this path is a delta, always moving,
like time, that touch
on the deep quietness
in a brief moment.

Brief, this floating-
time; brief
its spinning journey
in ever-coiling labyrinths,
seething uncertainties, flames,
and transparent
complexity.

TRAZO DEL TIEMPO

Entre el viento y lo oscuro,
entre el gozo ascendente
y la quietud profunda,
entre la exaltación de mi vestido blanco
y la oquedad nocturna de la mina,
los ojos suaves de mi padre que esperan; su alegría
incandescente. Subo para alcanzarlo. Es la tierra
de los pequeños astros, y sobre ella,
sobre sus lajas de pirita, el sol desciende. Altas nubes
de cuarzo, de pedernal. En su mirada, en su luz envolvente,
el calor del ámbar.
Me alza en brazos. Se acerca.
Nuestra sombra se inclina ante la orilla. Me baja.
Me da la mano.
Todo el descenso
es un gozo callado,
una tibieza oscura,
una encendida plenitud.
Algo en esa calma nos cubre, algo nos protege
y levanta,
muy suavemente,
mientras bajamos.

MARKS OF TIME

Between wind and dark,
between a rush of joy
yet deepest calm,
between my lovely white dress flying
and the dark, dark hole of the mine,
are my father's eyes, so gentle, waiting; his dancing
happiness. I go to meet him. This is a land
of little stars, of pyrite crystals,
wherever it's touched by the sunset. Clouds
of quartz, and flint, up high. His bright gaze,
all-embracing,
has the warmth of amber.
He lifts me up into his arms. He comes in close.
Our one shadow drifts over to the edge of the mine. He puts me down.
He gives me his hand.
The whole way down
is just one joy, in silence:
one dark warmth,
one richness, aglow.
Something in that quietness holds us under its wing, it protects
and uplifts us,
very softly,
as we go down.

DETRÁS DE LA CORTINA

Detrás de la cortina hay un mundo de calma,
detrás del verde espeso
el remanso,
la profunda quietud.
Es un reino intocado, su silencio.
Desde el espectro líquido
de otro mundo,
desde otra realidad de sonidos dispersos; desde otro tiempo
enmarañable, me llaman.

BEHIND THE CURTAIN

Behind the curtain there is a world of calm,
behind that thick green
is a peaceful place,
profound hush.
An unsullied realm, its silence.
From that flowing vision
of another world,
from that other reality's diaspora of sounds; from that other time,
enmeshed, they are calling me.

AGUA DE BORDES LÚBRICOS

Agua de medusas,
agua láctea, sinuosa,
agua de bordes lúbricos; espesura vidriante —Delicuescencia
entre contornos deleitosos. Agua —agua suntuosa
de involución, de languidez

en densidades plácidas. Agua,
agua sedosa y plúmbea en opacidad, en peso —Mercurial; agua en vilo,
      agua lenta. El alga
acuática de los brillos —En las ubres del gozo. El alga, el hálito de su cima;

—sobre el silencio arqueante, sobre los istmos
del basalto; el alga, el hábito de su roce,
su deslizarse. Agua luz, agua pez; el aura, el ágata,
sus desbordes luminosos; Fuego rastreante el alce

huidizo —Entre la ceiba, entre el cardumen; llama
pulsante;
agua lince, agua sargo (El jaspe súbito). Lumbre
entre medusas.
—Orla abierta, labiada; aura de bordes lúbricos,
su lisura acunante, su eflorescerse al anidar; anfibia,
lábil —Agua, agua sedosa
en imantación; en ristre. Agua en vilo, agua lenta —El alumbrar lascivo

en lo vadeante oleoso,
sobre los vuelcos de basalto. —Reptar del ópalo entre la luz,
entre la llama interna. —Agua
de medusas.
Agua blanda, lustrosa;
agua sin huella; densa,

WATER OF JELLYFISH

Water of jellyfish,
milky, snaking water
of ever-changing shapes; glossy water-flesh; melting
into its lovely surroundings. Water – sumptuous waters
receding, languid

and layered into calm. Water,
water silken, dusky, dense as lead – Mercurial; floating free,
    idling. The seaweed
in there, sparkling, in pleasure's very breast. The seaweed, crests a-bubbling;

– above the over-arching silence, above the long spits
of basalt rock; the water-weed, its familiar caresses,
its gentle flux. Water of light, of fish; the breeze, the agate
spilling its light. The shy elk flicker like flame

– Through the cotton-silk trees, through the shoals of little fish;
a flame is pulsing;
water slinking, lynx-like; water of bream (Jasper's sudden reds and browns).
Such glory here,
among the jellyfish medusas.
– Parted lips of coastline; the breeze's gentle movements,
lulling softly, settling into crystals, amphibious,
lubricious – Water, silken and
magnetic; poised. Water, coasting – Lascivious radiance

wading, oily,
over crumbling basalt. – Light, opal, crawls
through its own inner flames. – Water
of jellyfish.
Sweet fresh-water shine;
water leaving no traces; dense,

mercurial
su blancura acerada, su dilución en alzamientos de grafito,
en despuntar de lisa; hurtante, suave. —Agua viva

su vientre sobre el testuz, volcado sol de bronce envolviendo
—agua blenda, brotante. Agua de medusas, agua táctil
fundiéndose
en lo añil untuoso, en su panal reverberante. Agua amianto, ulva
El bagre en lo mullido
—libando; en el humor nutricio, entre su néctar delicado; el áureo
embalse, el limbo, lo transluce. Agua leve, aura adentro el ámbar
—el luminar ungido, esbelto; el tigre, su pleamar
bajo la sombra vidriada. Agua linde, agua anguila lamiendo su perfil,
su transmigrar nocturno
—Entre las sedas matriciales; entre la salvia. —Agua

entre merluzas. Agua grávida (—El calmo goce
tibio; su irisable) —Agua
sus bordes

—Su lisura mutante, su embeleñarse
entre lo núbil
cadencioso. Agua,
agua sedosa de involución, de languidez
en densidades plácidas. Agua, agua;   Su roce
—Agua nutria, agua pez. Agua

de medusas,
agua láctea, sinuosa; Agua,

mercurial
>   white as steel, parting round the granite stacks,
its flashes of minnows; secretive, smooth. – Water alive,

and rolling; a bronze sun vaulting in close;
– liquid minerals, spurting. Water of jellyfish, a water to feel
dissolving into itself
into a slick of indigo, quivering honeycombs. Long strands of water,
>   sea-lettuce,
The catfish nibbling
in its rich, streaming bed, whose light nectars
form a golden pond, liminal. Weightless water, air inside amber,
– a chrism of light, full of grace; the high tide a tiger,
below a wash of shadow. Water at the edge, water-eel, swallowing itself,
its great journey by night
– Along these matrices of silk, through the sea-sage. – Water

rich with hake. Heavy water (– That calm pleasure,
warm; the way it shimmers)
– Water's edge

– Its smooth changes, its delight in itself,
its own seductive rise and fall. Water,
silken, receding, layered
into languid calm. Water, water;   Its gentle stroke
– Water of the otter, the fish. Water

of jellyfish,
milky, snaking; Water,